tate publishing
CHILDREN'S DIVISION

LiFE
IS TOO
SHORT
TO BE
CHIC

ELIZABETH PIPES SWANSON

Published by Tate Publishing & Enterprises, LLC
127 E. Trade Center Terrace | Mustang, Oklahoma 73064 USA
1.888.361.9473 | www.tatepublishing.com

Tate Publishing is committed to excellence in the publishing industry. The company reflects the philosophy established by the founders, based on Psalm 68:11,
"The Lord gave the word and great was the company of those who published it."

Book design copyright © 2015 by Tate Publishing, LLC. All rights reserved.
Cover and interior design by Cecille Kaye Gumadan

Published in the United States of America

ISBN: 978-1-63306-400-3
Poetry / General
15.03.02

This book is dedicated to God who made
me his private stenographer. And to
all the souls who read this mystical
musing, and gleam a particle of
something for their magical lives.

Hold your breath
Wish upon a star
Wink
Cry
Hold a hand
Tell a story
And
Never stop loving, and saying so
Never lose your roots
Your heritage
And
Your precious sense of humor

So...

Sleep in your bathing suit

Paint your own toenails

Play dress up

Write a love letter...and mean it

Collect shells

Overstay the sunset

Sing out loud in the shower...Louder

Cut a bunch of flowers

Plan your own funeral

Learn pig Latin

Make homemade fudge

Drink a real Coke

Call an old boyfriend

Enjoy coach. You don't have to
upgrade to have a good time

Ride the bus, train,
streetcar, or trolley

Walk

Pray

Wear sneakers. Honor your feet

Wear your hair in pigtails

Chew bubblegum

Make Jell-O and add Cool Whip

Eat with a plastic spoon

Eat a lot of peanut butter

Linger over an old magazine

Explore many thrift shops

Write a short story

Plant sunflowers everywhere

Skinny-dip

Run away for a day (tell no one)

Take up the hem

Learn to sew

Needlepoint, embroider, cross-stitch, and darn

Speak Spanish anyway. You can!

Why?! Who cares? Who Says?

Have you called your mother today?
Collect pennies

Share your jewelry—costume and real

Scatter your trinkets
Instead of thank-you notes,
just write
Don't send flowers...Paint a picture
Tell your secrets

Tell the truth

What is your secret?
Believe
Trust
Compliment
Grow up
Shape up
Grow old and become younger
Dance often
Dance daily
Tap dance
Sleep naked
Sleep on the patio under the stars
Graft a rose bush

And so...

Have a slumber party
Wear flip-flops—the people's choice
Do you know a good podiatrist?
Stand in line at the US Post Office
with the rest of us mortals
Whenever...order doughnuts
Cry a lot...like a baby
Forget the calories...grams of fat

Slip into church and light a candle
for the world
Sing gospel
Play golf with a tennis racket
Hop on a plane without a reservation
Travel with carry-on only
Meet by accident

Believe in fate
Visit a cemetery with a bouquet,
note, or stone.
Wash your car
Wash your hair
Wash your soul

Call a friend from long ago

Miss her

Miss him

Miss them

Stop and hear the ocean

Remember your dreams, forget your
nightmares

Eat all alone

Find your first-grade teacher

Find a hero

Find a heroine

Find hope

Make peace

Watch out for rainbows

Catch a mosquito hawk...Let it go

Catch a moonbeam...Let it go

Oh, eat a Snickers

Perform a ritual

Make your grandmother's favorite
homemade jelly, pot roast, or stew

Go fishing

Try camping

Stay up all night

Thank Frank Sinatra

Visit the Holocaust Memorial Museum, Washington, DC

Write to the president, write him anyway

Listen to Lena Horn sing "Lady Is a Tramp"

Applaud

Become a romantic

Wear lace

Be forever in blue jeans

Be an idealist

Be real

Be authentic

Be tacky

Be grateful

Go back to your roots

Lose the phony accent

Find your father

Don't wear black for a week

Stop grieving

Stop!
Play jump rope, jacks, and
pick-up sticks
Chew more bubblegum
Take a bubble bath
Sleep in a hammock

So...
Go on a picnic
Thank and hug a tree
Save a frog
Help a turtle cross the road
Rescue a helpless bumblebee from a
swimming pool
Wave to a construction worker
Honk to a handsome dude
Kiss all of "it"
Fall asleep with a gardenia
in your hair

Dream the impossible
Do you know what's possible?
Miracles are possible

Pray again
Long for something
Ache for the broken heart of a friend
Stand and serve in a soup kitchen
Give up

Surrender
Change your mind
Change your heart

Change a diaper (in a nursing home)
Stop screening your calls…Pick it up
Tech, heck…I've had it!

Breathe
Retire your panty hose
Build a sand castle
Go to the movies alone
Avoid the shopping outlets on a
beautiful day
Reminisce
Call the old boyfriend back

Put the tweezers down
Say no to café latte

Get addicted to something healthy
and wonderful

Fall in love again, again, and again

Walk in the moonlight alone

Be a godmother

Take your aunt to dinner

Spend the weekend with your
grandparents

Spoil your parents

Make a fuss over your cousins

Help someone carry their groceries

Complain

Complain and be heard

Fight

Disagree

Be patient

Be attentive

Stop! Listen to the silence

Have a scavenger hunt

Win first prize in anything

Ask a stranger to dance

Run…Don't jog

Climb a tree—not a mountain

Prolong your sorrow

Learn to mourn

Drive your convertible with the top
down in the rain

Call the radio station...Request your
favorite song

What is your favorite song?

Kiss him...Kiss him anyway

Hold hands

Write poetry with your left hand

Howl with your dog

Thank your pets

Feed the birds

Feed your soul

Cry without abandon

Go homeopathic

Thank the wrinkles

on your face

Smile at strangers

Walk in the rain...Who cares about

your hair?

Jitterbug to Elvis's "Hound Dog"

Slip into a bologna sandwich

Make friends with mayonnaise

Paint a hibiscus flower in technicolor

Forget your sunglasses

Wear your eyes

Don't wear a bad suit

Show your arms

Flaunt your waist

Like your profile

Change your perfume

Change your hair

Change your mind

Chase a butterfly

Keep up with a hummingbird

Kiss a lot of frogs…One has to be a prince

Find a prayer group, temple, synagogue, and mosque

Get a blood test

Vacuum

Iron

Whistle

Hum your favorite tune

Learn to cook with cumin

Try out for a play, forget about
your butterflies

Make fresh lemonade

Use only one credit card

So try cash. You need it!

Plant plastic flowers on your
pet's grave

Believe in miracles

Believe in something

Anything

Beg for passion

Beg for compassion

Beg for commitment

Beg for second chances

Beg to be taken back

Take someone back
Take out the garbage
Stop calling your cat
Stop looking for your glasses
Give the trainer a break
Give up the gym
Pierce your ears
Pierce your heart
Sit through a movie twice—at
least till you get it
Don't rely on your horoscope
Don't be with a psychic
Have faith
Play Monopoly, gin rummy, and strip
poker…It's revealing

Be familiar with your opponents
Perfect your poker face

Buy six lottery tickets, give them
all away
Send a friend flowers—anonymously
Dry your clothes on a clothesline

So...

Forget the mousse for your hair
Forget your hair
Don't wear a watch, buy a sundial
Tie a ribbon in your hair
Pull the bangs off your face
Put on a triple coat of mascara

Bat your eyelashes
Tie a piece of string a round
your finger,
so you don't forget who you are

So who are you anyway?
Who cares? Who says?
Be late
Apologize...often
Explain
Communicate
Empathize
Be aware
Be present
Be able

Clean out the back of your car

Thank Abraham Lincoln, George
Washington, and Jimmy Durante

Surprise yourself

Don't polish the silver

Let your old cashmere be finished off
by the moths

Finish the conversation

Confide in the moon

Build a teepee and crawl inside

Harmonize

Play a harmonica

Cancel your haircut…let it grow!

Wear a tiara and skip work

Pack a picnic for yourself

Mow your lawn, mow your neighbor's
lawn

Say grace before a meal

Forgive Rhett Butler

Pray for Scarlett

Sell those damn curtains
immediately!

Read in French, do it anyway

Why?! Who cares? Who says?
Bite your nails...Rip off the fakes

Be startling real
Tell the truth
Fall out of love
Fall in love
Break a date
Write some more poetry
Clean out your drawers, throw out
your underwear
Blow up your fifth-grade photo
Learn the butterfly stroke
Feed the ducks in the park
Buy a swing
Swing weekly
Catch a fish
If you catch it, clean it please
Cook it

No goldfish allowed

And So...

Leave the quarters in the pay phone

Sit on the front steps
Sketch on the back steps
Wear gloves
Wear your class ring
Buy a corsage
Relive your wedding
Relive your life...where is the joy?
Propose marriage
Play Old Maid
Drink milk at bedtime with
Ginger Snaps
Short sheet the man in your life
Sing a camp song...Remember it
Build a campfire
Take up the ukulele
Take a vacation...play and stay home
Wear a slip
Reread Cinderella
Put out the cigarettes
Easy on the hooch
Don't panic
Give up your temper

Patience is power
Laugh and act up
Open a window…inhale hope
Plan a bake sale
Nap on the grass
Play hard to get
Hike
Row
Design in beads
Play Dominos
Spy on porpoises

Still be afraid of snakes
Learn to drive a motorboat
Finger paint
Bake cookies from scratch
Play hopscotch
Take a hose bath
Buy a birdbath
Raise chickens
Move away

Start all over again
Get a new doctor, but not too many

Thank your old doctor

Go to the fair and ride the carousel

Play darts

Learn to shoot pool

Teach your dog new tricks, and you too

Read the Bible...the longest-running best seller

Set your alarm for 5:00 a.m. get up and journal

Make potholders

Write a short story, now publish it

Take singing lessons

Play badminton

Play dolls

Play cowboys

Marry a cowboy

So...

Live on a ranch

Live happily ever after

Adopt a child

Be adopted
Like your in-laws
Thank your mother-in-law
Be positive
Be polite, always
Be sensitive
Be true
Behave
Be still
Be silent and reverent
Be good
Be kind
Be beloved
Be real and forever
Be wise
Be triumphant
Be noble
Be generous

Be humble
Be yours (always)

Be gracious
Be honest

Be sincere

Be mine

Be romantic

Join something, join everything

Act goofy, act silly

Pitch a fit—especially for ice cream

Call your mama

Call your papa

Write a speech

Change your major

Change your career

Change the color of your hair

Take off the braces

Thank your parents

Go on a diet

Go off the diet

Cuddle and snuggle, spoon and squeeze

Faint

Surrender gently

Be kind, not right

Wear jodhpurs

Ride a horse

Neck whenever possible
Go to a drive-in movie
Clap out loud for yourself
Practice your Oscar acceptance speech
Be Miss America (for a day)
Sing Opera...Try again
Play the piano

Allow a panic attack
Don't panic
Squeal
Giggle
Holler
Speak the truth

So...
Take a cold shower

Allow your heart to break open
Break a couple of eggs for breakfast

Kneel, bend, and bow
Sleep alone...with courage
Rise to meet the evening star
Wish on a shooting star

Unplug the blow dryer…Use rollers
Read Elizabeth Barrett Browning's
"How Do I Love Thee?"
Play spin the bottle
Detox
Concentrate
Focus
Don't interrupt

Interrupt politely
Marry a man who cooks
So, do you wear a girdle?
Fire the TV
Love the weather

Await all seasons
Stop controlling
Embrace carbohydrates
Risk it all
Sleep late
Hooray for yoga and Pilates classes

Keep Friday night free
Cry at airports

Stare at phenomena
Marvel at magic
Put your therapist on a
leave of absence
Boogie
Don't be cool or aloof
Be available
Be vulnerable
Be nervous
Be alert
Tell fairy tales
Believe in fairy tales
Tell stories. What's your story?
Design a party dress
Enjoy your own party
Listen
Listen
Listen

Scramble from scoundrels, scandals, and shenanigans

Remember, love happens

Death happens

Birth happens

Divorce happens

Marriage happens

War happens

Transformation happens

Tragedy happens

Second chances happen

Adultery happens

Celebrate

Meditate

Don't overmedicate

And So...

Demonstrate

Crack your veneer

Have second helpings of life

Believe in Santa Claus, the Easter Bunny,

and Prince Charming

Eat a regular diet of popcorn, peanuts, and cotton candy

Recapture your youth

There's life after monogram stationery

Feel yourself

Vote—you better!

Daydream...a lot

Buy a hamster

Don't live beyond your means

Love your neighbor

Forgive your enemy

Forgive yourself, often

Choose love and not money

Don't social climb

Slow dance

Lead with your heart

Emulate yourself (only)

Tell your child who you really are—

Who are you anyway?

Adore, cherish, appreciate, and protect your children

Above all, teach your children the
example of love and faith

Swallow your pride whole, like your
vitamins

Trust beyond a doubt

Reject nothing

Travel South

Submerge yourself in New Orleans

Can you swim?

Visit the dazzling decayed Cuba

Envy Tina Turner's spirit

Never forget Princess Diana

Stop rationalizing

Embrace your freckles

Spend time with a veteran

Allow your hair to turn gray

Answer an ad in the newspaper

Tear up your script—ad lib

Promote yourself…hourly

Answer the questions honestly

Sleep in a motel under a flashing
neon sign

Don't be afraid to talk and snore in your sleep

Fry chicken, livers, gizzards (no lizards)

Make eggnog year-round

Leave a packed suitcase by the front door

Get goose bumps, chills, and butterflies

Hit the beach

Trust your cleaners, but not with your wedding dress

Fast once a week

Be a lady

Be a gentleman

Be an icon (to the poor)

Be anonymous

Champion the runt

Believe in centrifugal force, synchronicity, and miracles

Marry a pirate and get used to his ship

Carve your loved one's initials on a tree
Win a trip to Paris

So...
Fight plastic on an ongoing basis
Fight for your children

Fight for your country
Fight for yourself
Drive stick shift
Rake leaves
Wash windows

Dare to reinvent yourself
Swim upstream in a hot flash
Don't get ulcers
Be unassuming
Be modest
Don't be vain
Reject terminal narcissism
Enjoy a traffic jam
Turn off the Walkman

Pay attention

Rely on your intuition
Depend on your instincts
Carry a flashlight and a spare key
Play hide and seek…Get caught

Be firm, in spite of the cellulite
Be baptized
Be holy
Acknowledge and respect
your depression
Waltz. Tango. Samba. Mambo. Jitterbug
and Merengue in your living room.

Take lots of photographs. Don't pose
Make friends at the Laundromat
Examine your conscience

Invest in yourself, more

than the market
Share your lunch with a
homeless person
Champion the Red Cross
Give hand-me-downs to the

Salvation Army
Deliver "Meals on Wheels"

Order a cheeseburger with extra,
extra everything
Stop living the illusion
Let a tear stain your cheek

Let your lower lip quiver
Be a good sport
Be a good student

Lady, be good
Yearn to be accepted for who you are
Thank your lawyer, no more deals

Close the door, leave

open a window
Apologize
Make a fuss over your waiter
Tip generously
Compliment the chef
Eat at a soda fountain
Run from your enemy and straight into
the arms of your dreams

Pardon your pain
Be light, not dark
Detox your brain
Refrain

Try it again
Amen, sister!
Hallelujah, brother!
Thank ya, Lord!
Visit the zoo…Who are you?
Pay your loans
Pay back often

So... So...
Pay attention
Notice everything
Read, read, read
Be a ballerina
Be a philosopher
Be somebody
Be yourself

Be!
Rest assured

Rest your laurels
Rest at peace
Count your blessings
Count your friends
Count your white lies
Let your imagination wander
around the block
Create your life
Choose your life
Protect your life

Live your life with urgency
Grace
Blow a kiss good-bye

Always look straight into their eyes
Don't be afraid to fall in love
Encourage everyone
Criticize nothing
Exalt the universe

Pray for vision (without glasses or
contact lenses)
Overwhelm him

Snow her
Show them
Perpetuate integrity
Serve pork chops
Serve with no expectations
Serve your country
God Bless America!
Fly the American flag!
Collect stamps

Buy a ball gown, hitchhike

to the ball
Buy a real Christmas tree and wreath
Buy only real
Be authentic
Be courageous

Be

Be with your friends at death
Bury your friends
Honor your health
Don't be hung up on wealth
Economize—get a roommate

Teach anyone anything

at any time

Explore your closet, garage, and mind

Imagine yourself broke

Imagine yourself begging

Imagine yourself homeless

Imagine yourself

Imagine yourself rich

Imagine love

Imagine

Imagine hope

Imagine faith

Godspeed

Don't speed

So...

There are no coincidences

You are the exception

Never give up

Win or lose, don't play games

Play hard

Run faster...to your goals

Be a good sport
Turn up the heat
Adhere to your promises
Remember Moses had a stutter

Remember Peter betrayed Jesus three times
Visit the West Coast of Florida in July
Find a soul mate
Mate with your soul

Excavate your soul
No excuses
What are the solutions?
Take a risk...several times a day
Be in awe of Sophia Loren
Be paranoid, for what?
Awake...at night
Send postcards always
Maybe yes and maybe no

Do you get it?
Make a goat your friend
Follow a seagull along the beach
It's okay! Okay?
Have you had your grits today?
Grits not Polenta
Square dance more

Be wiser than you are
Pretty is as pretty does…maybe?
Avoid permanents, collect bobby pins
Admire a fireman
Buy if you must
Sit through a thunderstorm
Don't be afraid of lightning
There is only today

What are you pretending

not to know?

Don't compromise (hardly ever)
Barbecue every so often
Invest in a jukebox
Swoon over jazz
Forget the shortcuts
Buy fresh produce
Are you a closet bacon eater?
Be homesick
Flirt to maximum capacity
May I please?
With permission
Sincerely yours
Many thanks
With kind regards
See ya soon
Thank you so much
Muchas gracias
Deep appreciation
Computer...give it a break
Typewriter...use carbon paper

So...

No more crumbs

Ask for more

Plead sanity

Avoid congestion—bodily and
environmentally

Be patient with your mother

Allow your brothers and sisters to be
your best friends

Forgive your parents

Love both of them

Follow your passion anywhere

Hold hands on the first date

Kiss on the last date

Don't forget your rouge or lipstick

Wink

Smile

Avoid lists

Show respect

Save nothing. Use it up

Bid the "persona" good-bye

Announce your loneliness

Elope

Hit Broadway…It's never too late

Regret not being a Girl Scout

Be wholesome

Rent "furnished," build new memories

No more delusions of grandeur

Lavish love

Help the hopeless

Tie someone's shoelaces

Obliterate bigotry

Abhor treason

Forgive, and learn from the past

Allow yourself to be held

Kiss

Say "I love you"

Marry again, please

Hurry up, and don't wait for the raise

Conquer your husband with kisses, backrubs, and pizza

Compliment his clothes

Eagerly await your birthday
Remember the cottage with
the picket fence exists
Picket!
Protect your skin…Use a parasol
Be visible
Be audible
Be eccentric
Be full of character
Be impulsive
Don't be compulsive
Don't postpone disappointment
Propagate possibility
Take "nothing" for granted,
especially "everything"
Scream out loud
Cancel the madness
Like Motel 6, keep your light on
Be luminous

Don't settle—ever
Do you believe in reincarnation?
Bless you

Be amidst angels
Be anointed in grace
Be faithful and await fruition
Carpe diem
Tempus Fugit
Adios
Dios

And happily live your life with
no regrets

e|LIVE

listen|imagine|view|experience

CPSIA information can be obtained at www.ICGtesting.com
Printed in the USA
LVOW02s0033020915

452476LV00007B/10/P